Consolation Prize

poems by

Tyler Robert Sheldon

Finishing Line Press
Georgetown, Kentucky

Consolation Prize

Copyright © 2018 by Tyler Robert Sheldon
ISBN 978-1-63534-628-2 First Edition
All rights reserved under International and Pan-American Copyright Conventions. No part of this book may be reproduced in any manner whatsoever without written permission from the publisher, except in the case of brief quotations embodied in critical articles and reviews.

ACKNOWLEDGMENTS

With gratitude to the editors of the following publications, in which these poems, often in earlier versions, first appeared:

Kansas Authors Club – "In Which You Wake Up"
I-70 Review – "Brother" and "Scar"
The Midwest Quarterly – "Gravity"
Thorny Locust – "Discovering a Lost Twin"
Tin Lunchbox Review – "OBE"
"Waking after the Wreck" first appeared in *Traumas* (Yellow Flag Press, 2017).
"Consolation Prize," "Post-Trauma," "OBE," and "After a Crash" were also featured in the MFA thesis exhibition "Chronicle & Character," by Taryn Möller Nicoll, at Louisiana State University. These poems accompanied her artwork about trauma survivors undergoing surgery. My endless appreciation to Taryn for including my work in her exhibition, and for providing this chapbook's excellent cover art.

Publisher: Leah Maines
Editor: Christen Kincaid
Cover Art: Antidromic: Ambiguus. Copyright© 2017 by Taryn Möller Nicoll
Author Photo: Copyright© 2018 by Alexandria Arceneaux
Cover Design: Elizabeth Maines McCleavy

Printed in the USA on acid-free paper.
Order online: www.finishinglinepress.com

Author inquiries and mail orders:
Finishing Line Press
P. O. Box 1626
Georgetown, Kentucky 40324
U. S. A.

Contents

Consolation Prize 1

With Full Intent of Distraction 2

Finding Home 3

Brother 4

Post-Trauma 5

Knockout Gas Sonnet 6

OBE 7

Discovering a Lost Twin 8

Waking After the Wreck 9

Scar 10

After a Crash 11

Space-Time 12

Gravity 13

In Which You Wake Up 14

*For my spouse and partner, Alex Arceneaux,
the finest poem I know.
For my brother, Cody William Sheldon. I think of you daily.
And for those who have survived.*

Thanks always to my family, who helped me find my way toward these poems.

"For it is important that awake people be awake . . .
the darkness around us is deep."

—William Stafford, "A Ritual to Read to Each Other"

CONSOLATION PRIZE

After Grandmother's chemo
her hair came back like cinnamon,
how she wore it at twenty, thirty.
At the piano she looked younger,
back straight, fingers dancing
on the black and ivory keys.

Only later came the gray tank of air
she needed to get through her day.
She wheeled it from room to room
and it squatted by her rocking chair.
In the sixties many nurses smoked,
a habit she had polished like a badge.

Grandpa had traded smokes for peppermints
back when. He got thinner. He brushed his teeth
more often. Grandmother got thinner too.

They sent letters every few weeks.
They said everything was good.
The new doctor was the best they'd had
in years. Grandmother's dusty voice,
always bouncing, told me she stayed
young because she wanted to.

When she threw away her cigarettes
Grandpa brought her a jar
of peppermints in cellophane wrappers.
They learned slowly to empty the jar
together. They brushed their teeth
more often, a habit they kept
polished like a badge.

WITH FULL INTENT OF DISTRACTION

If this is on purpose you have nothing
to be ashamed of. Acid will do that
to your skin occasionally, and
people are going to take you
more seriously now. This
is something you can't change.
Don't try.

Why do you insist on wearing plaid.
You know bees swarm and attack
more frequently those who
wear plaid. Is it to distract
from what the acid has done
to your skin.

The bees will only make this worse.
They will begin to hive
under the muscles of your arms.
You will not be able
to smoke them out.

When your teeth
begin to buzz from the
movement of wings
up the ladders of your shoulders
You will realize you need
the bees there.

They will distract from how
the acid has mottled your skin.
You will vibrate down-street
and relearn slowly how
to be happy.

FINDING HOME

Any cold sweats in the early morning
are only ever a dream. Pay no attention to how
the nervous twinge of adrenalin makes you
run for any dark room and sit there for hours.
When, in darkness, you bolt your teeth
around a pillow know that others around you
are doing the same. Their day too has been
the worst anyone has ever experienced.

But know that if you find unspoiled anything
in your refrigerator it has been a good day.
If you trip on the sidewalk and catch yourself
at the last moment it has been a good day
because you're not in the hospital
and can read this poem. If you're hit by
rain en route home sans umbrella
it has been a good day because you can feel
the world talking around you. You can
splash into puddles and follow that rain.

BROTHER
for Cody

"...able to touch your heart like a leaf."
—*Jimmy Santiago Baca*

You, with the cluster of hospital tubes
held too loose in your premature blood,
your small felt hat in a closet box
that squats out of sight like a fist.
You, who left me breathing alone.

You, sitting in Peter Pan Park
in leaf-scattered morning sun.
You, whose spinal fluid broke all rules
and made its own cranial walls.
You, whom I will always understand
just as well as myself, and not at all.

I feel you in the back muscle twinges
that cling me to bed in the morning.
I see you behind my eyelids, and touch
you as I pluck a leaf from concrete
when my left hand is free.

POST-TRAUMA

The invisible hands that lace tight our nerves,
that hold us after the dark god-bombs come—
bombs that fall heavy through our upcast eyes—
we call these hands the Entity, and they
wait for us to call them forward.

The hands know that sinking below consciousness
is normal, our greatest bomb shelter.
They hold us still until we are ready to move
on our own. They flex our stolen legs,
stand before us on spread fingertips like armor.

The hands with their great green thumbs
garden our bodies with gentle rains.
We erupt in flowers the shade of new skin
and the frequency of hesitant heartbeat.

We learn to walk these gardens
with arms out to the rain. One socked foot
slides forward. We learn to balance
with our hands.

KNOCKOUT GAS SONNET

I never chewed bubblegum as a child.
All surgery masks held that acrid smell:
Chemicals to calm children, always wild,
least willing to give up control.

After surgery for rebellious teeth
I wrote "thank you" on my hand
for the anesthesiologist. I tried to speak.
My mouth was a cave of dark blood.
My hand would have to do.

Sometimes my tongue calls back
the fluorescent tang of latex gloves:
what hospitals smell like. A calling card
to show what we lack and how
we're always only fixed up for now.

OBE

> *"...an unusual group of experiences occasionally reported by some people awakening after general anesthesia."*
> —Australian anesthesiologist G.M. Woerlee

In the operating room where we learn
about cold metal and the flavors of gas,
a surgeon saves his first patient
finally from some malady (we
also learn the man's family had
prepared a tombstone) and collapses
to the table like a lung. The patient
will resurface soon. He knows
exactly how the surgeon's eyes
flickered like lamps, full
with half-lit fire. He breathes
not a word to anyone, but floats
above his doctor's shoulder,
last actor in a dark theater
where the curtain holds itself up.

DISCOVERING A LOST TWIN
for Cody

When a giant shark comes to you
in the night, glowing and shrieking
that ocean mammal binary

that you don't know logically,
but can somehow still connect with
on some hidden level of the amygdala,

is your first impulse to swim
away? Would you listen as it tells you
it's here to save you from drowning

in the dark ocean that suddenly
and ominously surrounds you?
Would you grasp for its pale fins

as it pulls you toward light?
Would you try simply
to wake up?

WAKING AFTER THE WRECK
Hutchinson, Kansas, 2012

Lady cop knocked
on cracked eggshell windshield,
mouthed, can   you   get out?

Pried driver door open over
broken airbag yolk. Across
the street the big truck rumbled,

driver pacing dark pavement;
passenger slumped in their seat,
crumpled, asleep.

Back of my car
undercarriage tumbled easy
into nighttime Kansas street.

SCAR
for Cody

At school, the other boys
mock me in the freshman
locker room.   I tell them
I'm the bionic man. They
know only how to breathe
through lungs that opened
and closed like bellows
since the day they were born.

In physical therapy, I learn
to ignore it through sit-ups
that stretch it like a smile
at my side. Later

I embrace it, run fingers
along puckered rib-skin
in the shower, breathe
deep because I can,
because through my ribs
is the metal holding tight
my lungs, the best hospitals
could do for a boy born
too early for much other
than prayer. While my scar

is still here, my brother
(three hours long for
our world) became his own,
spinal fluid scalding
his broken brain. It

reminds me memories
don't fade with age,
and some stretch to fit
the holes we make
in our hearts.

AFTER A CRASH

How ambulances lapse
                into silence
    (not doctor visits
        or cat scans or therapy)
after air bags
        knock you to sleep
    in the driver's seat

how a truck fender
        can fold a door in
              like foil
    and can spill your car
toward the only
        culvert in town
           without a fence

(how now you flinch
    each time anyone
        turns left, stoplight
    or not toward you)

that whistle (really a scream)
        is how you sound
when others hear you
    only once the steaming car
              is stopped

only once the cops
        pry open your door
    can you hear your voice
        again for the first time

            like a kettle on fire

SPACE-TIME
for Cody

The tiny ache of stars in the middle-landscape
of cold space isn't too unlike the incubators
in the NICU of a Midwestern hospital—
everything we see is flipped. We picture stars,
these plasmic spheres, X number of light years

removed, the ultimate self-propelled machines,
but really their pulsing hasn't happened in years.
The stars were gone long before any imagery
could capture them. And those incubators

described so often as vessels for premature hope
suspend for just a while our belief in space-time:
death surely cannot happen here, not with so many
doctors, tubes, crossed fingers.

Whenever the tiny fires inside burn out
we touch their slackened fingers
fold and pack their tiny clothes
and feel them echo outward
through centuries of sky to reach us.

GRAVITY

The chortle some birds make when afraid to fly
before their parents boot them to the ground for the first time
and they piece together that they'd better figure this out quick
isn't laughter but instead
realization that the world hates waiting.

Swifts, ocean birds that stay up
for years at a time and sleep on the wing,
don't ask how it all works because
maybe if they did it wouldn't anymore
and thousands of birds would fall
like comets into the sea.

No matter how they try
                      some birds can't fly.

IN WHICH YOU WAKE UP
after Albert Goldbarth

In those sparse gray moments
when you're half-awake
or else when you've been out
all night and it's not dawn exactly

but that soupy static half-light
of insomniacs and writers,
consider that you are still here. I don't mean
in your house or the bar or hotel room

where you've crashed (where
you're reading this poem),
but that you are alive,
part of that pre-dawn static

higher than our cilia can recognize.
Consider that you didn't make it, and instead
you're crisping away in an alternate universe
where someone just set the house on fire.

How does one deal with that sort
of heavy knowing: possibly
you're just one of nine lives (maybe
cats are trying to tell us something), and

you're already down to the
seven other yous, since that last one
didn't handle himself all that well?

Maybe your invisible other life smolders
away in that skeleton of a house, but
why would that be worth mentioning?

Tyler Robert Sheldon is the author of the poetry collection *Driving Together* (Meadowlark Books, 2018) and the chapbooks *Traumas* (Yellow Flag Press, 2017) and *First Breaths of Arrival* (Oil Hill Press, 2016). His poetry has been nominated for the Pushcart Prize and the AWP Intro Journals Award, and he received the Charles E. Walton Essay Award in 2016. His poems and book reviews have appeared or are forthcoming in *The Los Angeles Review*, *The Midwest Quarterly*, *The Dos Passos Review*, *Quiddity International Literary Journal*, *Pleiades*, *Coal City Review*, *The Prairie Journal of Canadian Literature*, *Tinderbox Poetry Journal*, and other venues. Sheldon holds a BA and an MA in English from Emporia State University, is an MFA candidate at McNeese State University.

Sheldon also teaches English Composition, and is a licensed English tutor through the College Reading and Learning Association. He enjoys playing guitar, wheel-throwing, printmaking, kayaking, engaging in literary criticism, and passing slower vehicles on the I-10 Corridor. He lives in Baton Rouge with his spouse and creative partner, the artist Alexandria Arceneaux.

www.ingramcontent.com/pod-product-compliance
Lightning Source LLC
LaVergne TN
LVHW041526070426
835507LV00013B/1843